NEEDLE FELTING
with cotton and wool

Jennifer Kooy Zoeterman & Linda Lenich

Martingale®
& C O M P A N Y

Needle Felting with Cotton and Wool
© 2008 by Jennifer Kooy Zoeterman and Linda Lenich

That Patchwork Place® is an imprint of
Martingale & Company®.

Martingale & Company
20205 144th Ave. NE
Woodinville, WA 98072-8478 USA
www.martingale-pub.com

Printed in China
13 12 11 10 09 08   8 7 6 5 4 3 2 1

Library of Congress Cataloging-in-Publication Data
Library of Congress Control Number: 2007041248

ISBN: 978-1-56477-796-6

CREDITS

President & CEO — Tom Wierzbicki

Publisher — Jane Hamada

Editorial Director — Mary V. Green

Managing Editor — Tina Cook

Developmental Editor — Karen Costello Soltys

Technical Editor — Carol Thelen

Copy Editor — Melissa Bryan

Design Director — Stan Green

Assistant Design Director — Regina Girard

Illustrator — Laurel Strand

Cover & Text Designer — Shelly Garrison

Photographer — Brent Kane

MISSION STATEMENT

Dedicated to providing quality products
and service to inspire creativity.

DEDICATION

To all the quilters, sewers,
needleworkers, and crafters whose
work continually inspires us.

ACKNOWLEDGMENTS

Thank you to all our family and friends for the
freedom and encouragement you have given
us to make this book possible.

Special thanks to our editor, Carol Thelen, and
to the staff of Martingale & Company for their
help, support, and talent.

CONTENTS

INTRODUCTION

Needle felting is a simple technique that you can use to add color and texture to your wool projects. Needle felt any shape or color by using a barbed felting needle to push colorful wool fleece, also known as roving, into the wool background fabric, causing the fleece to entangle and stay in place. Since the release of our first book, *Needle Felting: Simple Techniques, Beautiful Projects,* we've continued experimenting with needle felting using wool fleece. We have discovered new ways to quickly add needle-felted touches to our projects and quilts.

We're quilters who have worked in a quilt shop, so of course that means we have stashes of beautiful cotton fabric! Wonderful prints and stripes simply called out to be included in our wool needle-felted projects and quilts. We found that they fit right in. We developed new ways to use fleece to appliqué the cottons without threading a needle. Those prints looked great peeking out in reverse appliqué. Those stripes looked wonderful pieced into the borders and backings. Why keep those wools and cottons apart? They look charming together.

In this book we have had fun combining the rich color and texture of wool fabric and needle felting with the cotton print and striped fabrics we love so much as quilters. We hope that this second book will take you along with us, using this fast technique to add new needle-felted appliqué to your projects and quilts.

Whether you're a beginner or an advanced stitcher, we encourage you to learn new needle-felting techniques and to try your hand at adding them to everything from simple pincushions and pillows to more intricate table mats and small quilts. Circles, flowers, and pinecones can all be appliquéd easily without threading a needle!

Welcome to the creative and colorful world of needle felting with wool and cotton. Enjoy creating these items with all your favorite things, including wool, cotton, needle felting, and embroidery. We hope you'll try some of these new ideas and take a few creative liberties!

NEEDLE-FELTING TOOLS AND SUPPLIES

Needle felting is a simple technique of attaching wool fleece to background fabric using a barbed felting needle. The repeated up-and-down motion of the felting needle pushes the wool fleece into the background fabric. The barbs of the needle cause the fibers of the fleece to become entangled with the background fabric and stay in place.

A colorful assortment of wool fleece and wool background fabric used for needle felting

WOOL FLEECE AND WOOL YARN

Wool fleece is the natural fiber from sheep after it has been cleaned, carded, and dyed. Different breeds of sheep produce different qualities of fleece. Our favorite is merino wool fleece because it is soft and silky with a long fiber, making it an excellent choice for needle felting. The extra softness of merino wool makes it easy to direct the pliable fibers with your felting needle, allowing well-defined edges and details. And the silkiness of merino wool gives a smooth, neat texture to your needle-felted projects.

Wool fleece accepts dye beautifully and produces stunning colors. The wide color range provides a full artist's palette.

Needle felting with wool yarn makes creating vines and tendrils extra easy. When selecting wool yarn for needle felting, the yarn should have a loose twist. The wool fibers should be long, soft, and pliable. Our favorite is merino wool yarn.

BACKGROUND FABRIC

For hand needle felting, it is important to use 100%-wool fabric for the background, either off the bolt, hand dyed, or overdyed. All projects in this book use 100% wool as a base for the needle felting. Other fibers (nylon, silk, polyester, and so on) in the background wool can interfere with the process of hand needle felting, making the interlocking of fibers less secure.

For machine needle felting, background fabrics can be either 100% wool or wool blends, because the sewing-machine attachment has many needles and the machine provides enough speed and power to completely interlock the wool fibers. It is always a good idea to test the fabric before committing to a large project.

FOAM WORK SURFACE

For hand needle felting, we use a foam base that is 2" to 3" thick and approximately 12" square. The reusable foam work surface gives the needle a cushion to press into and protects the table as you needle felt.

HAND-FELTING NEEDLE

A hand-felting needle has no eye and is 3" long with very small barbs (notches) near the tip. The barbs grab the wool-fleece fibers and interlock (entangle) them into the fibers of the wool background. This single needle has two uses: it places fleece in position lightly and precisely (similar to pinning or basting), and it can also be used to secure wool fleece completely by hand.

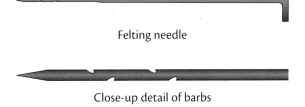

Felting needle

Close-up detail of barbs

Small barbs at the tip of the hand-felting needle entangle the fleece fiber into the wool background fabric on a foam working surface.

SEWING MACHINES AND NEEDLE FELTING

Several manufacturers offer sewing machines designed just for needle felting. These include Baby Lock Embellisher and Janome Xpressions. There are also needle-felting attachments available for certain sewing models of Bernina, Brother, and Pfaff machines. Check with your local dealer or online.

A multibarbed needle-felting attachment for the sewing machine will needle felt with more speed and power than felting by hand. In our method, we lightly needle felt by hand and then remove the project from the foam work surface. We place the project on the bed of the machine and complete the needle-felting process using a machine needle-felting attachment.

We've needle felted for years without Bernina's Needle Punch attachment, but now that we have one, we find that it's a valuable time-saver in the needle-felting process. Although helpful, a machine attachment is not a necessity for making the projects in this book.

A less-expensive option that works well is Clover's Needle Felting Tool and Mat. This is a hand-powered, multibarbed tool you use with a brushlike base instead of a foam work surface. Again, use of this tool is not mandatory for the projects in this book, but it is a time-saving way to complete the needle-felting process after your design has been lightly worked in with a single needle.

TECHNIQUES IN NEEDLE FELTING

Needle felting is a simple process; you can quickly learn both the basic and special techniques needed to make any of the projects in this book. After creating the basic shapes, use the special techniques to give them added dimension, texture, and color.

POSITIONING WOOL FLEECE

Needle felting lightly allows you to audition your design, almost like basting. You are free to change your mind about color, shape, blending, and positioning. When lightly needle felted, the wool fleece can be pulled off and put back in the bag for future use. Don't worry about creating exact replicas of our needle-felted designs; you're creating an artistic impression. If the colors and shapes are close enough, your design will look accurate. You can add more wool-fleece shapes or change their position and color. Go ahead—take a few creative liberties!

You can position your wool fleece by sight or mark the background fabric for exact placement. Placing by sight is a relaxed and uncomplicated method with no marking required. We like to place the fleece by eye because doing so requires no extra tools, saves time, and allows creativity and freedom in design.

If you prefer to have a clearer idea of where to place the fleece, use a chalk pencil to mark the background fabric. Lay the paper pattern on the background fabric. Lift a corner of the paper and mark key features of the design, such as the top, middle, bottom, and the position of the main shapes.

BASIC NEEDLE FELTING

1. Place the foam work surface on your table and lay the wool background fabric on top of the foam.

2. Hold the wool fleece lightly in one hand; with the fingertips of your other hand, gently pull off a small amount from the end. Keep your fingertips a few inches apart as you pull. If your fingertips are too close together, the long fibers will not release easily. Don't cut the fleece with scissors, because the cut fiber ends may not completely needle felt. Wool fleece goes a long way, so pull less than you think you need and add more as you go.

3. Place the wool fleece in the desired position on top of the wool background fabric. Hold the needle near its middle, between your thumb and forefinger. Keep your other hand away from the needle tip. Use the needle tip to move the fibers into the desired shape.

4. Push the upright needle through the fleece, into the wool background fabric, and down into the foam with a firm but gentle up-and-down motion.

5. Needle the wool-fleece shapes lightly at first. This is similar to basting and allows you to remove or reposition the shapes if you change your mind about color or placement. There is no waste with wool fleece.

6. Once you are pleased with the shape, color, and placement of your wool fleece, finish needle felting by hand or machine until the shapes are secured in place. Completed needle-felted shapes have crisp edges with very few, if any, visible stray fibers.

7. Remove the background fabric from the foam work surface. Turn it over and you will see the fleece fibers underneath.

CREATING BASIC SHAPES WITH WOOL FLEECE

Our technique of needle felting shapes from wool fleece allows you to determine size and shape, define points, blend color, and add dimension and texture.

Circle Flowers, Dots, and Berries

Pull a small amount of wool fleece and gather it into a loose ball with your fingers or palms. Place the ball on the wool background fabric. Lightly needle the ball in place by pushing the needle into the center of the ball and through the base fabric a few times. Using the needle, gather up stray fibers and push them into the center. Needle around the outside edge to define the circle shape.

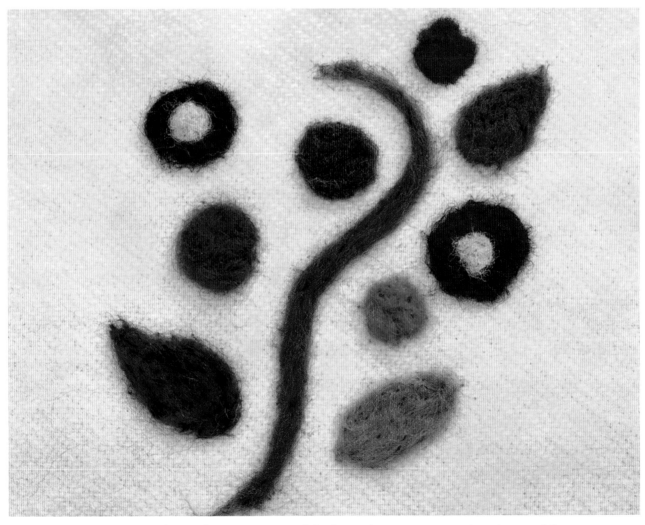

Leaves, stems, circles, and vines are some of the basic shapes you can make using wool fleece.

Stems, Vines, and Tendrils

Pull a length of wool fleece and lay it in position on the wool background fabric. If the pulled length or width is too short or narrow for your vine or stem, add fleece as needed to increase it. You can reduce the length or width by folding the fiber back onto itself. Needle the length lightly in place, and then needle the edges to define the shape.

Leaves and Petals

The two basic shapes used to make leaves and flower petals are the eye shape and the teardrop shape. Use the methods described below to begin forming the wool fleece into each shape. After shaping as described, place the shape onto the background fabric, lightly needle the center, and then define the points and edges to complete the needle felting.

Eye shape: This shape is pointed on both ends and round in the middle. Pull a small amount of wool fleece and pinch both ends.

Teardrop shape: This shape is pointed on one end and rounded on the other. Pull a small amount of fleece, fold it in half on top of itself, and pinch the unfolded end.

Needle-Felted Template Method

This method is useful in several different situations:

- When you want an exact shape of a design element to be needle felted in place

- When you would like to repeat a motif and want those motifs to be similar in size and shape

- If the shape is larger than 2"

Templates can be made of paper, cardboard, or quilter's template plastic. Trace the pattern onto the material of your choice and cut it out on the drawn line. Purchased plastic templates such as assorted sizes of circles, ovals, and leaf shapes can also be used.

1. Lay the background fabric on your foam work surface. Pull enough fleece to lightly cover the area on the background fabric where you want the template positioned. Lay the template on top

of the fleece. The fleece should extend beyond the edges of the template. With a felting needle, poke the fleece all around the edge of the template.

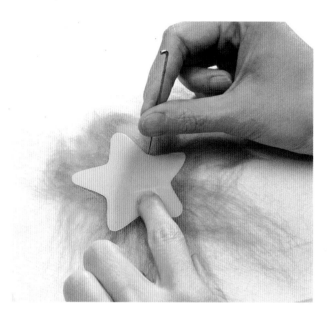

2. Remove the template and you will see the indentation line of the template shape.

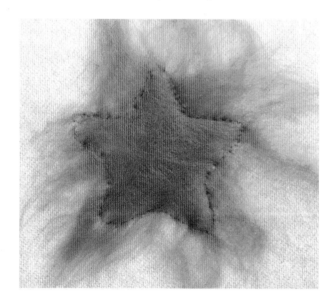

3. Using the edge of the felting needle, fold the stray fibers of fleece extending beyond the indentation line toward the shape.

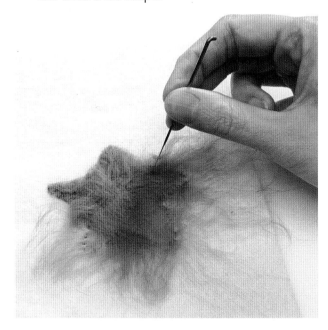

4. Fill in the shape by adding more fleece, if necessary, and needle felt completely.

COLOR-BLENDING TECHNIQUES

Wool fleece colors are beautiful right out of the package, but you can blend, highlight, and shade your own custom color combinations, just as a painter would mix colors on a palette. Mixing can be done before or during needle felting, or after the shape is completed. Remember that you can always change your mind and remove your choices, so don't let color blending intimidate you. Have fun and experiment!

Blend colors before needling. Pull the colors you want to blend and mix by layering them one on top of another, pulling apart, and then layering again. Repeat until the desired color blend is achieved.

Mix colors by repeatedly pulling apart and layering the wool fleece before shaping and needling.

Blend colors while needling. Lightly needle felt one color in position on the background fabric, add other colors on top, and lightly needle again.

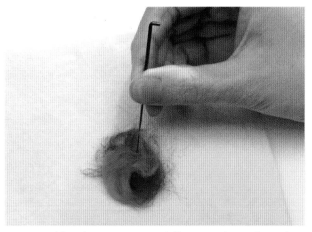

You can blend two or more different colors of wool fleece as you lightly needle first one color and then another.

Highlight and shade after your shape is created. Once your shape is completely needle felted, needle white or light colors over the top to add highlights. Highlights bring those parts of the shape forward. To shade, add black or dark colors to your shapes, making them seem to recede into the background.

Add light colors to give highlights to a shape.

DIMENSION AND TEXTURE TECHNIQUES

Forming dimensional shapes in various ways is another delightful feature of needle felting.

For a flat appearance: Needle your entire wool fleece shape until it becomes flat and compact. The shape will look almost level with your background fabric because the fleece fibers are so deeply imbedded.

For a raised, compact appearance: Add more layers of wool fleece to the shape and needle felt each layer until you get the desired height. Introducing more layers of fleece will raise the shape above the background fabric.

For a sculpted, lofty center with deeply set-in edges: Needle the edges densely, leaving the center of the shape less needled for a loftier look. Berries and petals will have a rounded, dimensional look.

For a sculpted, indented center with lofty edges: Heavily needle the center to push it deep into the background fabric, leaving the edges lightly needle felted. Use this technique to define leaf veins in detail.

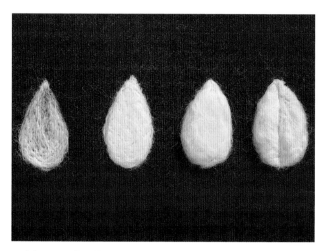

Add several different levels of dimension to your needle felting. Left to right: the yellow shapes are flat, raised, sculpted with a lofty center, and sculpted with lofty edges.

NEEDLE FELTING ALLOVER DESIGNS

Needle felting an allover design can turn a plain wool background into a spectacular one. To create needle-felted stripes, simply lay fleece or yarn randomly in lines. For a free-form approach, randomly place squiggles or stippling of yarn or fleece on the background fabric. Position the yarn or fleece in place and needle felt into the fabric.

A solid background fabric can be easily changed into an interesting fabric by needle felting wool yarn or wool fleece in a random pattern.

NEEDLE-FELTED APPLIQUÉ

Needle-felted appliqué is our technique of using fleece and the basic needle-felting technique to attach pieces of wool, cotton, or both onto a wool background fabric.

Attaching pieces of wool or cotton fabric to your wool background fabric can be done easily by placing a dot of fleece in the center and then needle felting right through the layers. No thread is needed to secure them in place. This method adds a three-dimensional quality to your quilt or project, and is a quick way to create elements such as pinecones and flowers. We never had this kind of fun with traditional appliqué.

Needle-felted centers attach cotton and wool fabric shapes to the background fabric.

WOOL APPLIQUÉ

Wool appliqué is easy because the cut edge of tightly woven wool doesn't fray—this means no seam allowances to turn under. The small amount of fraying that you get with loosely woven wool is generally not a bother. This wonderful quality also lets you cut your own rickrack and free-form strips for stems and vines. Various embroidery stitches will easily hold the appliqués in place and add even more color and texture detail. Finish up by including needle-felted details, and discover how your wool appliqué projects and quilts can take on a whole new look.

CHOOSING WOOL FABRIC

Select 100%-wool fabric that's off the bolt, hand dyed, or overdyed. Medium-weight wool is the easiest to cut and appliqué. Avoid lightweight gabardine because it will be too slippery; conversely, blanket-weight wool will be too heavy. Look for tightly woven wool so the cut edge won't fray. Sometimes gorgeous, loosely woven wool can't be passed up. When that happens, we don't let a little fraying brother us. *Note:* Some wools will need to be felted (shrunk) before use. This is explained in the next section.

FELTING WOOL

Hand-dyed and overdyed wools are felted and ready for use. Many high-quality, off-the-bolt wools are woven tightly enough that they do not fray and can be used without felting. If there is some fraying and you want to remedy this, you can felt (shrink) the wool in your washing machine. Felting or shrinking 100%-wool fabric is simple. To protect your washer and dryer from getting clogged with lint, place your wool in a large, zippered pillowcase. Place the pillowcase in the washing machine with hot, soapy water. Agitate for a full cycle and rinse with cold water. Dry in a hot dryer, cleaning the lint trap often.

WOOL RICKRACK

Cutting wool rickrack is just a variation of regular rotary cutting in which being meticulous isn't required. Choose wool fabric that is tightly woven or has been felted (see "Felting Wool" above). You will need a wave-blade rotary cutter and a wave blade. For some projects in this book, you will also need a scalloped blade. (Check to see whether the wave or scalloped blade you choose will fit the cutter you already have. Depending on the brand, some blades might require a specialty cutter.)

Make the first cut using a ruler as a guide. Because the wave could nick your ruler, don't press the blade directly against the ruler as you would do with a straight blade. Cut slowly with even pressure. Move the ruler over ¼" from the peak of the first cut and make a second cut. As you begin this cut, try to line up the valleys and peaks. The wave may not stay in alignment, which is fine; simply choose the rickrack strips with the best cuts for your project.

Cutting wool rickrack with a wave blade

Appliqué over the rickrack from valley to valley using pearl cotton with a long straight stitch.

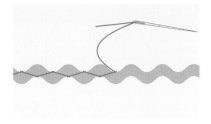

Appliquéing wool rickrack

CUTTING FREE-FORM STRIPS

You can easily use a rotary cutter or scissors to cut freestyle, making gentle curves and varying the desired width from thick to thin. No need to use a ruler!

To appliqué free-form stems, embroider with a straight stitch, cross-stitch, or blanket stitch using pearl cotton.

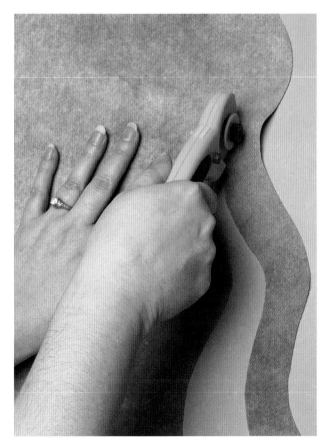

Cutting free-form strips with a straight blade

FREEZER-PAPER TEMPLATES

When it comes to appliqué, wool has no right or wrong side. The grain line can be ignored, so you can show off the fabric's plaid, stripes, or color shades in hand-dyed wool. The fact that there is no added seam allowance means you can cut on the drawn line.

1. Trace the pattern onto the dull side of the freezer paper. Cut out the freezer paper ¼" from the drawn line. Place the freezer paper, shiny side down, onto the right side of the selected area of fabric.

2. With a dry iron set on the wool setting, press the freezer paper onto the wool. Cut out the shape on the drawn line. Peel off the paper.

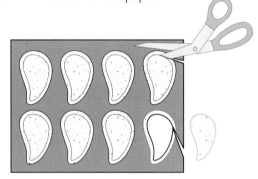

Freezer-paper templates

STITCHING WOOL APPLIQUÉS

We like to use a #22 chenille needle for appliqué- ing wool. It has a sharp point, and the eye is large enough to thread #8 pearl cotton. For appliqué thread, we love #5 or #8 pearl cotton in a wide range of solid or variegated shades. Pearl cotton's extra thickness prevents it from sinking into the wool. To add extra interest, use a thread color that contrasts with the appliqué. We are always amazed at how much a variegated pearl cotton can perk up an unin- teresting scrap of wool fabric.

For appliquéing, we use the blanket stitch or cross- stitch.

For added detail, after the appliqués are stitched in place, we also use decorative embroidery stitches over the wool appliqués and wool fleece. These stitches include the French knot, backstitch, running stitch, chain stitch, and stem stitch.

Blanket stitch

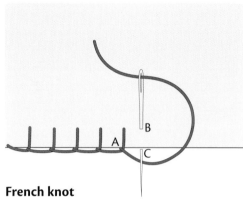

Cross-stitch

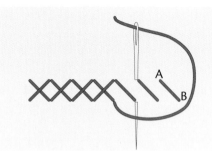

French knot

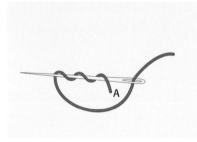

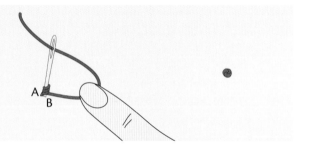

Backstitch

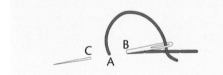

Running stitch

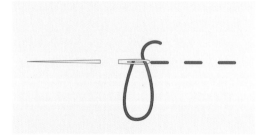

Chain stitch

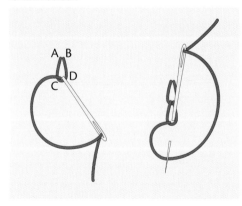

Stem stitch

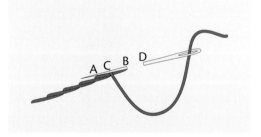

REVERSE WOOL APPLIQUÉ

Regular appliqué involves stitching fabric on top of fabric. Reverse appliqué involves cutting a window of any motif or shape in background fabric and stitching fabric under the background fabric. Using wool for a background fabric helps make this method easy. There is no turning under the edges because the cut window does not fray. To add interesting texture, cotton or wool fabric can be stitched under the background wool.

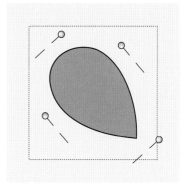

1. Make a template by tracing the pattern shape onto the dull side of freezer paper. Cut out the freezer paper on the marked line. Place the template onto the background fabric.

2. Mark around the template using a pencil on light background fabric or a chalk pencil on dark background fabric. If the wool background fabric is resistant to marking, position the freezer paper template, shiny side down, on the background fabric. Press in place with an iron on the wool setting.

3. With sharp, pointed scissors, cut out the shape on the drawn line or around the freezer-paper template to reveal the window.

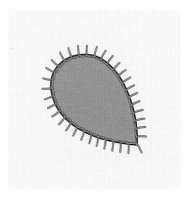

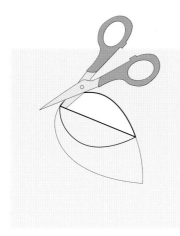

4. Cut a piece of cotton print or wool fabric larger than the window opening. Slip this fabric behind the cut window and pin in place. Using a blanket stitch or straight stitch, sew around the background fabric to hold the appliqué in place.

TIPS FOR PIECING WOOL

When piecing wool, it's best to use a ½" seam allowance. This wider seam allowance helps to keep the seam flat when it's pressed open. As a general rule, when working with wool we press the seams open. Here are some additional tips on piecing wool:

- When pressing wool, use the iron's wool setting to prevent scorching.
- Because of wool's thickness, it is helpful to use a walking-foot attachment on the sewing machine.
- We lengthen our stitches to seven to nine stitches per inch. Large stitches make a smooth seam and make ripping seams from wool much easier.
- Sew a little slower than usual.
- When cotton and wool fabrics are sewn together, sometimes they stretch at the seam. Just use a rotary cutter to straighten the edge.
- Avoid sewing tiny wool pieces together. Wool is best left in large, chunky pieces, which are easier to sew and press.
- It's fun to sew decorator fabrics to wool because they are a little heavier and can stand up to wool's weight.

FINISHING

After the quilt top is complete, you'll want to add quilting and binding to finish the project. We have included some special techniques to use when marking, quilting, and finishing your needle-felted wool quilt tops.

MARKING AND QUILTING WOOL QUILT TOPS

Marking wool quilts can require a little experimentation. Some wool will mark easily with a chalk pencil or quilt marking pen. Other wool will not be so cooperative; in this case we keep our quilting simple. We like to stitch in the ditch either by hand or by machine using a walking foot. If we are going to add straight-line quilting, we use masking tape as a guide for our quilting lines. We rarely use batting in our wool quilts, because they are thick enough without it. This makes the quilting much easier. For hand quilting we prefer a #22 chenille needle and #8 or #5 pearl cotton, which really makes the stitches stand out on the wool. Quilting thread gets lost in the loft of the wool, and we believe that if you are going to do handwork, it should be shown off. We pin baste our quilts. One thing to keep in mind is that wool can shift, so make sure your wool top is placed squarely on your backing fabric.

FOLD-OVER BINDING

We find that folding the backing fabric over to the top edge of the quilt is the easiest and quickest way to bind these projects. This technique requires the backing fabric to be cut larger than the quilt top. Choose a cotton or wool backing fabric that will coordinate with the quilt top. After you are finished quilting, use a walking foot to machine baste ½" from the edge of the quilt top to stabilize the layers. Trim the backing fabric 1" to 1½" wider along the edge of the quilt top. Each project will specify the exact measurement needed.

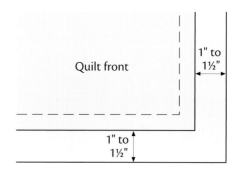

For cotton-backed quilts, we like a narrow binding. Cut the backing edge 1" beyond the quilt edge. Fold the raw edge to meet the edge of the quilt and press. Place the folded edge over the quilt-top edge to hide the basting stitches. Sew in place by machine, or by hand using the blanket stitch or running stitch.

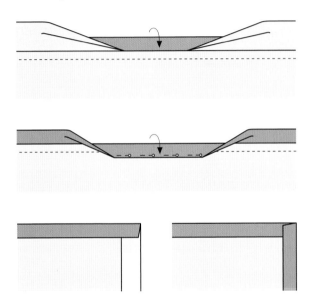

For wool-backed quilts, we like to show off the extravagance of the wool. Cut the backing edge with a scalloped-blade rotary cutter, leaving about 1½" beyond the edge of the quilt top. Each project will specify the exact measurement needed. When folded over the front edge of the quilt top, the scalloped edge of the backing fabric acts as binding and makes

a decorative edge. Fold over the backing to hide the basting stitches. Stitch in place with pearl cotton and a blanket stitch.

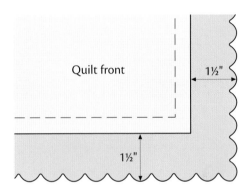

CLEANING AND PRESSING

Use a lint roller to remove any stray fibers from the background fabric. In most cases no pressing is needed, but if pressing is required, use a press cloth to prevent scorching and a steam iron set on the wool setting. If the shapes are flat, we use a steam iron and lightly press over the entire design. If the shapes are sculpted, we use a steam iron and lightly press around the needle-felted shapes or hold the iron a few inches above the fabric and give the shapes a shot of steam.

Wool doesn't need to be cleaned as often as other fibers because it repels soiling. If a wool item does need to be cleaned, hand wash it in cool water using a mild soap and then lay the item flat to dry. Washing doesn't change the needle-felted design.

POSY PINCUSHION

OUR GRANDMOTHERS KNEW THAT THE BEST PINCUSHIONS WERE
MADE OF WOOL. THIS PROJECT IS A GREAT WAY TO LEARN NEEDLE
FELTING WHILE CREATING A PRETTY PLACE FOR YOUR PINS AND
NEEDLES. GRANDMA WOULD BE PROUD.

FINISHED SIZE: 6" X 7"

MATERIALS

6½" x 7½" piece of pink wool for backing

5" x 6" piece of cream wool for top

Scrap of purple cotton print for large flower

Scraps of green, blue, yellow, and pink wool for leaves and flowers

Pure Wool Inc.'s 100% merino yarn and fleece/roving color palette pack in *Sweet Pea*

Hand-felting needle

2"-thick foam work surface

#22 chenille needle

#8 pearl cotton in green and purple

Straight pins

Polyester fiberfill

Scalloped-blade rotary cutter, cutting mat, and ruler

CONSTRUCTION

1. Using the patterns on page 24, cut one small flower from blue wool, one large flower from purple cotton, two leaves from green wool, and one flower center from yellow wool.

2. Round all corners of the cream wool piece with scissors. We simply eyeballed the rounding of the corners and didn't bother with a template.

3. Referring to the placement guide on page 24, pin the flowers and leaves in place. Follow the basic needle-felting instructions on page 11 for creating dots and circle flowers.

Fleece, wool, and cotton are dyed in a wide variety of colors. It's fun to play with your own favorite color combinations.

Place the yellow wool flower center on top of the purple cotton print flower. Needle felt pink fleece for the center dot and three small mint fleece dots to secure the flower to the cream wool top.

4. Needle felt a circle flower of purple and mint fleece in the center of the blue wool flower. Then needle felt a dot of light purple fleece in the center of the pink wool flower to secure it to the cream wool top.

5. Position the green wool leaves under the purple flower, extending them over the edge of the cream wool top. Pin in place. With pearl cotton and a running stitch, embroider along the center of each leaf, stopping ½" from the edge of the cream wool top.

6. Embroider a stem for the berries using pearl cotton and a stem stitch. Needle felt seven dots of purple and pink fleece to create berries. Follow the pattern for berry placement.

7. Using the scalloped-blade rotary cutter, trim all four edges of the pink wool fabric so that the piece measures 6" x 7". Center the finished cream wool top on the backing fabric and pin in place.

8. Stitch the pincushion top to the backing using purple pearl cotton and a straight stitch, leaving a 3" opening. Stuff the pincushion with fiberfill and continue to stitch closed.

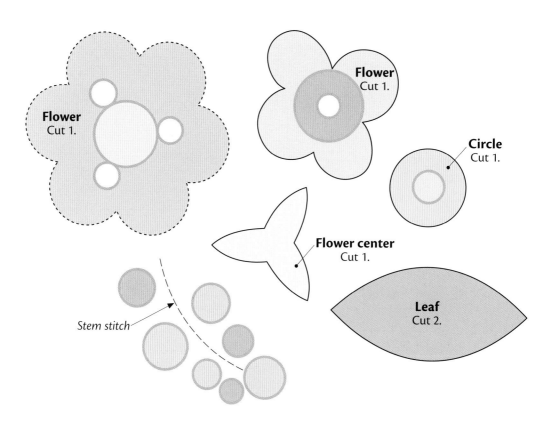

Flower
Cut 1.

Flower
Cut 1.

Circle
Cut 1.

Flower center
Cut 1.

Stem stitch

Leaf
Cut 2.

Patterns and placement guide

- - - - - - - - Cotton appliqué

———————— Wool appliqué

══════════ Felting

LEAFY PHOTO FRAME

THE WARM TOUCH OF WOOL AND COTTON SURROUNDS
A TREASURED PHOTOGRAPH, KEEPING YOUR MEMORIES
COMFY-COZY.

FINISHED SIZE: 8" X 10"

MATERIALS

8" x 10" piece of cream wool for background

Scraps of dark pink wool for leaves

Three 2" x 2" squares of blue cotton print for leaves

Two 1½" x 1½" squares of black wool for photo corners

Pure Wool Inc.'s 100% merino yarn and fleece/roving color palette pack in *Jewel Box*

Hand-felting needle

2"-thick foam work surface

#22 chenille needle

Sharp, pointed scissors

Freezer paper

#8 black pearl cotton

Straight pins

Wave-blade rotary cutter, cutting mat, and ruler

8" x 10" frame

8" x 10" peel-and-stick mounting board for textile art (found where embroidery, cross-stitch, and needle-point supplies are sold)

Photograph, approximately 3" x 5"

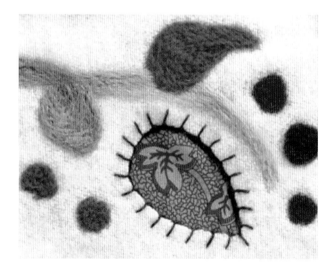

CONSTRUCTION

1. To make photo corners, cut each 1½" black square in half diagonally with a wave blade.

2. Use your photograph as a guide for placement of the fabric photo corners. Place your photograph 1" from the bottom and 1" from the right edge of the background fabric. Photo corners should be positioned ¾" from the edge of the background fabric, covering the corners of your photo. Pin corners in place. Using a chenille needle and pearl cotton, stitch a running stitch along the straight edges to secure the corners to the background.

3. Use the placement guide on page 28 for positioning the vine. All needle-felted shapes and appliqués are kept ¾" from the background edge. Lightly needle felt yarn in place for the vine.

4. Using the freezer-paper template method described on page 17, cut out three leaves of dark pink wool and pin them in place. Refer to the placement guide as needed. Needle felt a vein in the center of two leaves to secure them to the background fabric. With a chenille needle and pearl cotton, blanket stitch around the remaining wool leaf and use a running stitch to create a center vein.

5. Cut three leaf-shaped windows for reverse appliqué as described on page 19. Place a 2" square of blue cotton print under the leaf windows of the wool background fabric and pin in place. Using a blanket stitch or running stitch with a chenille needle and pearl cotton, stitch the blue cotton in place.

6. Refer to the photograph on page 27 for placement and color of needle-felted dots for berries. Needle felt two small leaves near the ends of the vine. When you are happy with their placement, completely needle felt the vine, berries, and leaves.

7. Secure the wool background fabric to the peel-and-stick mounting board, following the manufacturer's instructions. You may have to trim the background fabric to the edge of the mounting board to fit into your frame. Place in frame.

8. Tuck in your photograph behind the wool photo corners.

The versatile leaf design gives you the freedom to turn the project upside down or sideways to accommodate most photos. The photo corners make changing the photos easy.

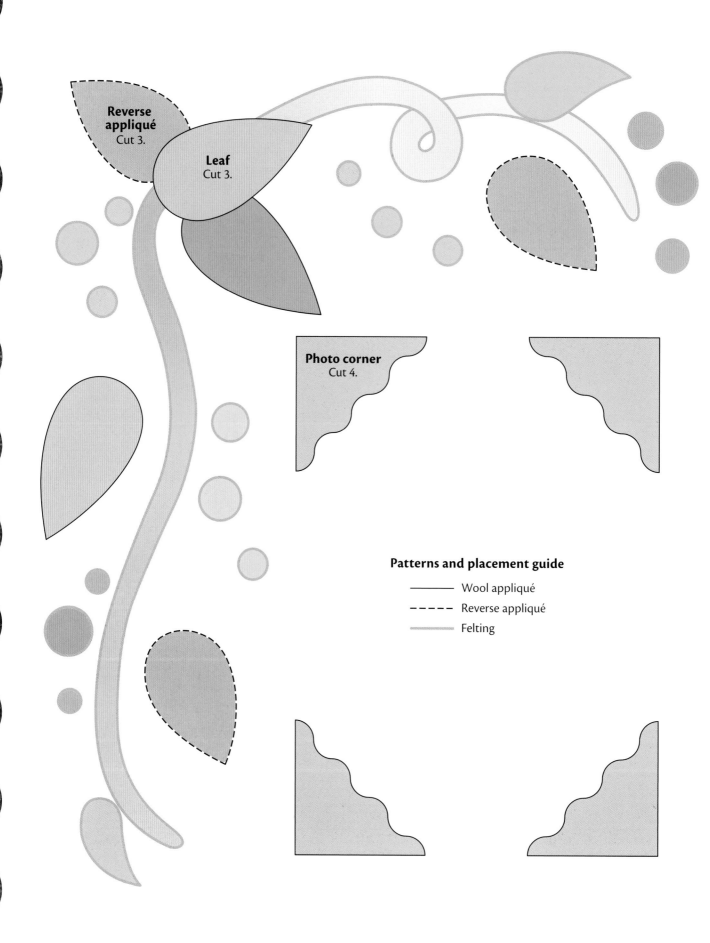

Reverse appliqué
Cut 3.

Leaf
Cut 3.

Photo corner
Cut 4.

Patterns and placement guide

——————— Wool appliqué

— — — — — Reverse appliqué

———————— Felting

BRIGHT AND HAPPY PILLOW

CREATE YOUR OWN NEEDLE-FELTED BACKGROUND FABRIC, AND THEN ADD
CHEERFUL FELTED CIRCLES USING OUR TEMPLATE TECHNIQUE.

FINISHED SIZE: 11" X 15"

MATERIALS

12" x 16" piece of green wool for background

1/3 yard of coordinating cotton for backing

6" x 8" piece of dark blue wool for circle background

1/4 yard of red wool for piping

Pure Wool Inc.'s 100% merino yarn and fleece/roving color palette pack in *Kindergarten*

Hand-felting needle

Straight pins

2"-thick foam work surface

#8 pearl cotton in green, yellow, blue, and red

#22 chenille needle

Straight-blade rotary cutter, cutting mat, and ruler

12" x 16" pillow form

Fiskars Shaped Templates in Circles (found in the scrapbook section of larger sewing stores or a scrapbook store) or 1", 1½", and 2" circle templates

CONSTRUCTION

1. To stripe the green wool background, gently divide the yarn in half lengthwise. Lay 9 or 10 strands of the yarn vertically on the green wool. Don't worry about making sure they are straight. Needle felt all strands of yarn in place. Cut off excess yarn at the edge of the green wool. To round the corners of the green wool background, mark curves using one of the larger circle templates or a coffee cup, and then trim with scissors.

2. Needle felt all the circles referring to the placement guide on page 32. To make circles on the dark blue background, use the "Needle-Felted Template Method" on page 12. Use the 1", 1½", and 2" circle templates. Layer the needle-felted circles starting with the largest circle. On top of the large circle, repeat the template method with a smaller template. Then completely needle felt the circles.

3. Using a chenille needle and pearl cotton, embroider cross-stitches and running stitches.

4. Position the dark blue wool fabric off-center on the green background, about 2½" from the bottom and side edges. Pin in place. Using a chenille needle and pearl cotton, blanket stitch the dark blue wool in place.

5. To make the red wool piping, cut enough 2"-wide strips to make the piping at least 50" long. Piece the strips together with a ½" seam allowance and press the seam allowances open. With wrong sides together, press the piping in half lengthwise.

6. Pin the red piping to the front of the pillow with cut edges together. Stitch ¼" from the edge to hold securely in place.

7. To make an envelope backing, cut the cotton backing into two pieces, 11'' x 12". Make a ½" hem along one 11" edge on each rectangle.

8. Place the green pillow top right side up and place the two cotton backing pieces on top right side down. Line up the edges so that they match the pillow top and overlap in the center. Pin the layers together. Trim the cotton fabric to match the rounded wool top. Sew together around all four sides using a ½" seam allowance.

9. Turn the pillow right side out and insert the pillow form.

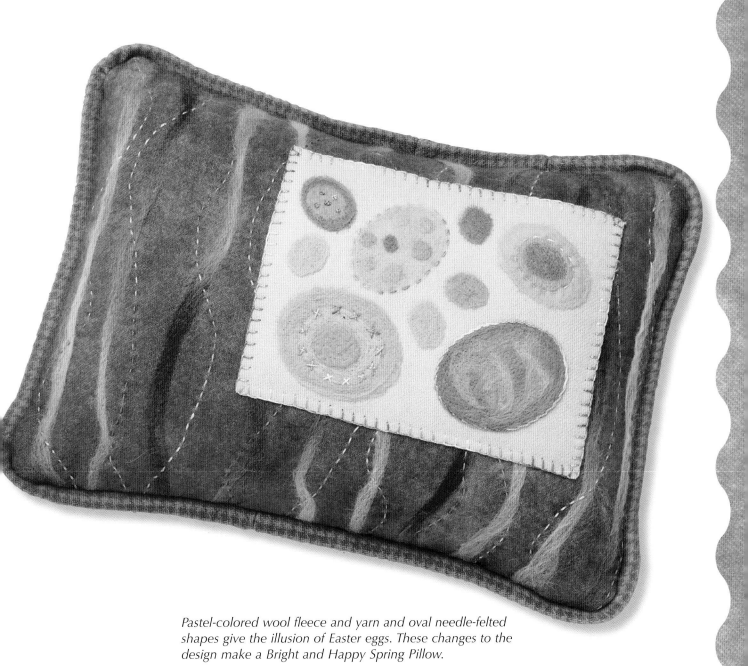

*Pastel-colored wool fleece and yarn and oval needle-felted
shapes give the illusion of Easter eggs. These changes to the
design make a Bright and Happy Spring Pillow.*

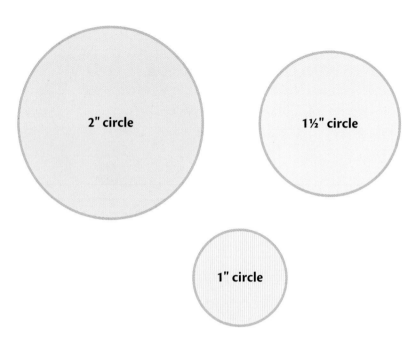

2" circle

1½" circle

1" circle

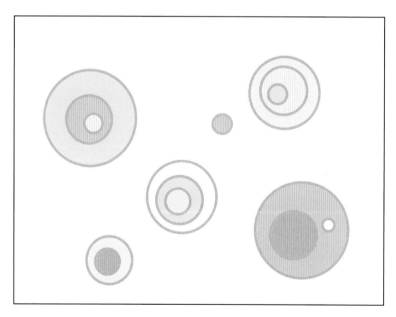

Patterns and placement guide

――――― Felting

CONFETTI AND STREAMERS NOTEPAD COVER

WOOL FABRIC, WOOL FLEECE, AND A COTTON LINING MAKE A DECORATIVE

NOTEPAD AND PENCIL COVER. KEEP IT BY THE PHONE TO JOT DOWN THOSE

LITTLE NOTES AND USE THE POCKETS TO HOLD RECEIPTS OR MAIL.

FINISHED SIZE: 9" X 12"

MATERIALS

10" x 13" piece of green wool for front

10" x 13" piece of cotton print for lining

7½" x 13" rectangle of coordinating cotton print for first inside pocket

4½" x 13" rectangle of another coordinating cotton print for second inside pocket

Scraps of green, red, pink, and cream wool for streamers and stars

Coordinating sewing thread

Pure Wool Inc.'s 100% merino yarn and fleece/roving color palette pack in Jewel Box

Straight pins

Freezer paper

½"-wide Steam-a-Seam 2 Double-Stick Fusible Web

Hand-felting needle

2"-thick foam work surface

Marking pencil or chalk marker

Sewing machine with zigzag capability

5" x 8" writing tablet

Wave-blade rotary cutter, cutting mat, and ruler

CONSTRUCTION

1. Referring to "Wool Rickrack" on page 16, cut a total of six 10" lengths from green, red, pink, and cream wool rickrack for the streamers. Cut one rickrack streamer from cotton fabric slightly wider than the wool strips. Position the streamers on the green wool, referring to page 36 for placement. Pin in place.

2. Using a sewing machine with matching or contrasting thread, sew a zigzag stitch on top of each streamer.

3. Make freezer-paper templates for the three star flowers using the pattern on page 36. Cut out the stars from the red, pink, and green scraps. Cut three ¾" squares of cream wool. Place them on top of each star. Referring to the placement guide, position the shapes and pin them in place.

4. Refer to "Basic Needle Felting" on page 10 and needle felt the stars with squares in place with a dot of fleece. Varying the dots' size and color, needle felt random dots along the streamers. Remove the pins.

5. To hem the two inside pockets, fold under ½" along one 13" edge and press. Secure the hem with fusible web, following the manufacturer's instructions. Place the lining and pockets as shown below with right sides toward the green wool front.

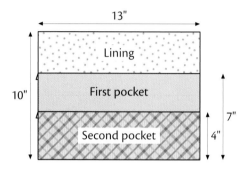

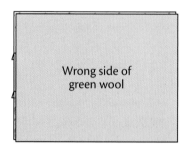

6. Using a ½" seam allowance, sew around all four edges, leaving a 4" opening on either side.

7. Clip the four corners and turn right side out.

8. Slip a piece of fusible web into the 4" opening and press closed.

9. Sew a straight stitch down the center of the cover and another row ½" from the right edge for the pencil holder.

10. Slip the notepad's cardboard backing into the upper-right pocket.

*Personalize your notepad cover with novelty cotton prints and coordinating
wool and wool fleece. The notepad is easily replaced after use.*

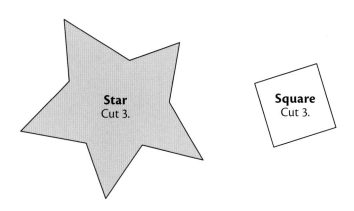

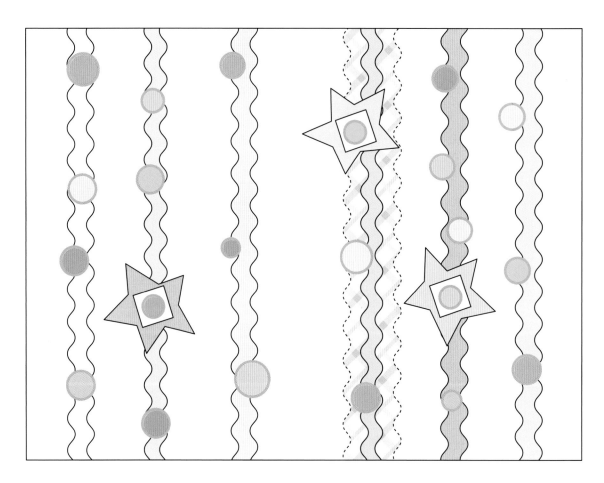

Patterns and placement guide

- - - - - - - - Cotton appliqué

————— Wool appliqué

⬝⬝⬝⬝⬝⬝⬝⬝ Felting

AUTUMN LEAVES WALL HANGING

CELEBRATE THE TURNING SEASON WITH LEAVES IN EARTHY COLORS, A BRIGHTLY

SHADED PUMPKIN, AND BOUNTIFUL ACORNS. NEEDLE FELTING WITH SHADES OF

BRIGHT ORANGE AND GOLD FLEECE HELPS TO CREATE THE FEELING OF FALL.

FINISHED SIZE: 15" X 20 "

MATERIALS

¾ yard of brown wool for background and backing with fold-over binding

Assorted scraps of wool and cotton prints for border

Green and orange scraps of wool for oak leaves

Pure Wool Inc.'s 100% merino fleece/roving color palette pack in *Golden Inspiration*

Hand-felting needle

2"-thick foam work surface

#22 chenille needle

Straight pins

#8 pearl cotton in colors to match or contrast with vine, leaves, acorns, and pumpkin

½ yard of green baby rickrack

Scalloped-blade rotary cutter, cutting mat, and ruler

CONSTRUCTION

1. Cut a 9" x 14" rectangle from the brown wool for background.

2. Refer to "Needle-Felted Template Method" on page 12 to create the pumpkin. Use the pumpkin pattern on page 41 and needle felt a pumpkin, centering it 1½" from the bottom of the brown wool background. After the pumpkin's shape is defined, give your pumpkin dimension by adding different colors of orange and gold fleece to highlight and shade. Needle felt a light brown multi-colored fleece stem to the top of the pumpkin.

3. Referring to "Wool Rickrack" on page 16, place the rickrack on the brown wool background. Trim the rickrack, if needed, and pin it in place. See the instructions on page 17 for stitching the rickrack with the chenille needle and pearl cotton.

USE PEARL COTTON TO YOUR ADVANTAGE

You can change the appearance of rickrack and other wool appliqués by adding a contrasting color of pearl cotton. For example, to tone down a bright shade of rickrack, stitch with pearl cotton in black or brown.

4. Use the freezer-paper method described on page 17 to make templates of the leaves on page 40. Cut out the leaves from the green and orange wool scraps. Referring to the placement guide, position the leaves and pin them in place. To attach the leaves, sew a running stitch along the center of each leaf and then blanket stitch around the orange leaf. On top of the green leaf, needle felt golden fleece accents for the veins.

5. Following the placement guide on page 41, needle felt the acorn using the tan fleece and multicolored brown fleece for the acorn cap. Acorns are circle shapes with half circles for the acorn tops. Shade and highlight as you wish. Using pearl cotton and a chenille needle, add embroidered details to the acorns.

6. Needle felt dots of orange, yellow, and gold along the vine, referring to the placement guide.

CUTTING FOR BORDER

From assorted wool and cotton fabrics, cut the border pieces as listed. All measurements include ½"-wide seam allowances.			
FABRIC	**PIECE**	**NUMBER TO CUT**	**DIMENSIONS**
Green cotton	A, K	2	4" x 5"
	O	1	4" x 4"
Orange wool	B, J	2	4" x 4"
	H, N	2	4" x 5"
Orange cotton	C	1	4" x 5"
Green wool	D, E	2	3" x 4"
	G	1	4" x 4"
Brown cotton	F	1	4" x 5"
	M	1	4" x 4"
Brown wool	I, P	2	4" x 5"
	L	1	4" x 4"

PIECING THE BORDER

1. Referring to the quilt diagram below, assemble the borders and press seam allowances open.

2. Referring to the quilt diagram below and the photograph on page 37, sew the pieced borders to the needle-felted block. Attach right and left borders first, and then add the top and bottom borders.

5. Use the binding method described on page 21. Use a scalloped blade to trim the brown wool backing fabric 1½" from the edge of the quilt. Fold the edges of the backing over to the top of the quilt edge and pin in place. With pearl cotton, blanket stitch the binding in place using the scalloped edge as a guide.

3. If your quilt top is uneven, trim the finished edges to make them straight and square the corners. Center the quilt top on the wool backing fabric, allowing 2" of backing around the edge to be brought around to the front for the binding. We did not use batting in this quilt. Pin baste.

4. Machine stitch in the ditch around the center block. For an accent, hand quilt with brown pearl cotton ¼" outside the center block. Hand quilt with brown pearl cotton around the pumpkin, vine, and green leaf. Add quilted details to the pumpkin as shown in the photo.

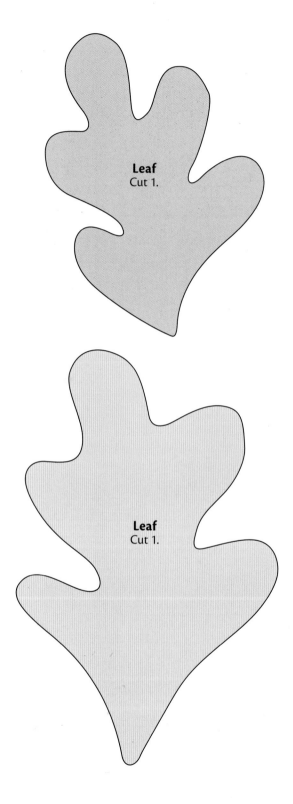

Leaf
Cut 1.

Leaf
Cut 1.

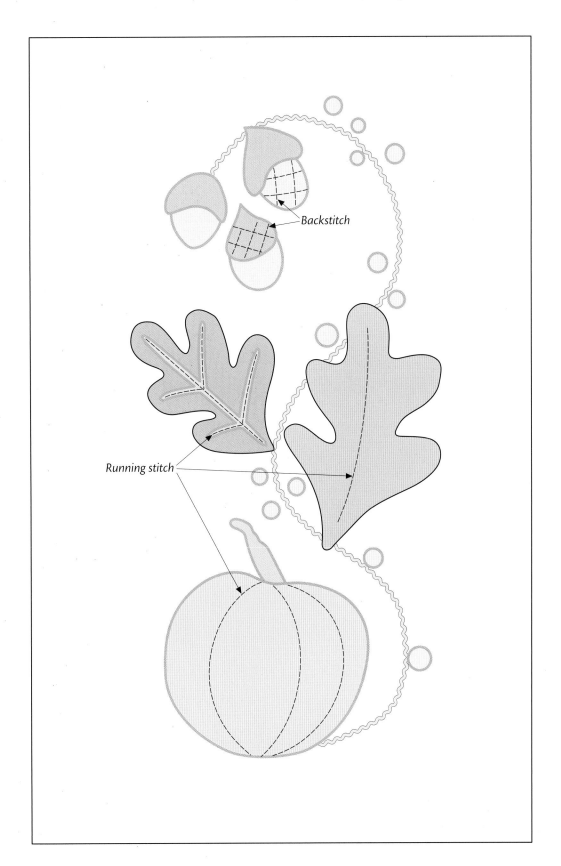

Backstitch

Running stitch

Placement guide

——————— Wool appliqué

〰〰〰〰 Felting

WINTER TABLE MAT

WINTER WON'T SEEM SO DREARY WITH THIS FRESH SPRIG OF PINE AND
POINSETTIAS TO BRIGHTEN YOUR TABLE. ONCE YOU LEARN HOW SIMPLE
AND EASY IT IS TO NEEDLE FELT A PINECONE, YOU WON'T WANT TO STOP.

FINISHED SIZE: 12" X 28"

MATERIALS

¾ yard of striped cotton

8" x 24" piece of green wool

1 fat quarter of dark green wool for branches

Scraps of brown wool for pinecones

Scraps of red wool and cotton for poinsettias

Pure Wool Inc.'s 100% merino fleece/roving color palette packs in *Golden Inspiration* and *The Classics*

Hand-felting needle

2"-thick foam work surface

#22 chenille needle

#8 pearl cotton to match or contrast with branch, poinsettia petals, and background fabric (The project shown used variegated green pearl cotton for pine sprigs.)

Straight pins

Rotary cutter, cutting mat, and ruler

CONSTRUCTION

1. Using the free-form strip technique described on page 17 and the green wool, cut two branches, ¼" to ¾" wide and in lengths of 18" and 21".

2. Referring to the placement guide on page 45 for positioning, place the stems and poinsettia petals on the green wool and pin in place.

3. Using matching or contrasting pearl cotton and a chenille needle, cross-stitch the branch in place. Use a running stitch along the center of the poinsettia petals.

4. To make pinecones, use the freezer-paper template method on page 17 and the patterns on page 46 to cut 27 shapes from brown wool—19 small, 6 medium, and 2 large. To create a pinecone, start by placing the tip of the pinecone small teardrop shape about 2" to 3" from the

branch. (See the placement guide on page 45.) Secure only the base of the wool appliqué by needle felting a dot of fleece. Then add two more small wool shapes, securing them in the same way and following the illustration below. Continue to add teardrop wool shapes and have the base of the pinecone end with the medium or large teardrop shapes. Don't worry about making exact replicas of ours.

5. With a stem stitch and variegated green pearl cotton, embroider pine sprigs, following the placement guide on page 45.

6. Needle felt red fleece dots for berries on the pine sprigs, shades of yellow fleece dots in various sizes for poinsettia centers, and white fleece dots for snow.

7. Cut two 12½" x 28½" pieces of the striped cotton fabric. Place them right sides together and machine stitch around all four edges using a ¼" seam allowance.

8. Carefully cut a 3" slit in the center of the top layer only. (The green wool fabric will cover the slit.) Turn right side out and press. Topstitch ½" from the edge.

9. Center the green wool on the striped cotton, covering the slit, and pin the wool in place. Using pearl cotton, blanket stitch the green wool to the striped fabric.

A pine branch with pine-cones was added to a soft, red wool purchased scarf. A second scarf for the lining was attached using a running stitch and red pearl-cotton thread.

44

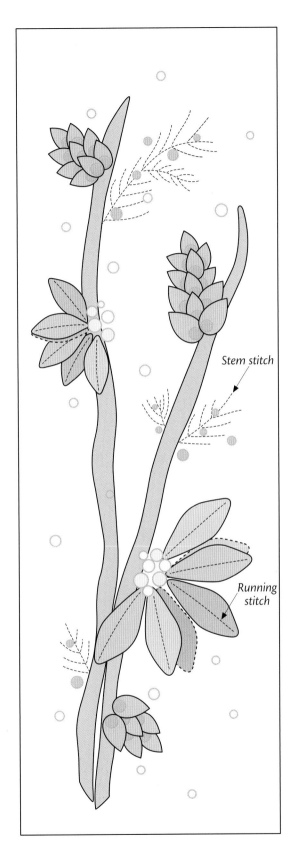

Stem stitch

Running stitch

Placement guide

- - - - - - - - Cotton appliqué

———————— Wool appliqué

———————— Felting

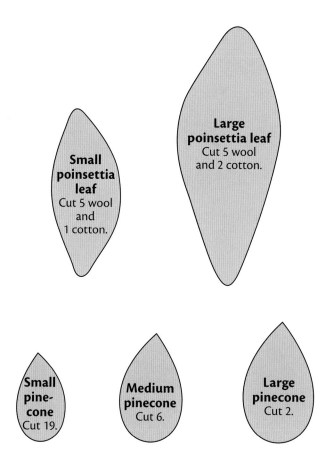

Small poinsettia leaf
Cut 5 wool and 1 cotton.

Large poinsettia leaf
Cut 5 wool and 2 cotton.

Small pine-cone
Cut 19.

Medium pinecone
Cut 6.

Large pinecone
Cut 2.

MIDGE'S HOLLYHOCKS QUILT

OUR FRIEND MIDGE GAVE US HOLLYHOCK SEEDS THAT BLOSSOMED INTO THE INSPI-RATION FOR THIS DELIGHTFUL QUILT. THEIR PERENNIAL BLOOMS OUTSIDE OUR SEWING-ROOM WINDOW REMIND US OF ALL OUR DEAR QUILTING FRIENDS.

FINISHED SIZE: 30" X 32"

MATERIALS

4 fat quarters of assorted green wool fabrics for flower stems and leaves

4 or 5 fat quarters of wool in shades of pale yellow, light blue, and medium blue for background

1 fat quarter of purple wool for lattice

Assorted scraps of wool and cotton prints for hollyhock flowers and leaves

1¼ yards of cotton for backing and fold-over binding

Pure Wool Inc.'s 100% merino yarn and fleece/roving color palette packs in *Red Rapture*, *Golden Inspiration*, and *Sweet Pea*

Hand-felting needle

2"-thick foam work surface

#22 chenille needle

#8 pearl cotton to match or contrast with flowers, leaves, and stems

Straight pins

Freezer paper

Wave-blade rotary cutter, cutting mat, and ruler

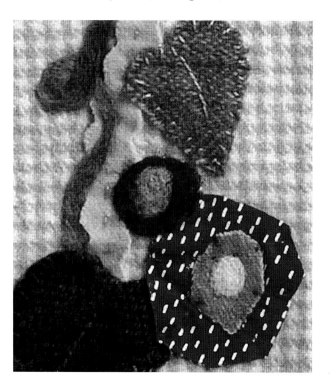

CUTTING

FABRIC	PIECE	NUMBER TO CUT	DIMENSIONS
All measurements include ½"-wide seam allowances.			
Medium blue background	A	2	5" x 21½"
	E	1	6" x 21½"
	I	2	5" x 9"
Purple lattice	B	2	3" x 21½"
	F	2	3" x 5"
	G	2	3" x 3"
	H	1	3" x 18"
	J	2	3" x 9"
Light yellow background	C	1	6" x 21½"
	K	2	6" x 9"
Light blue background	D	1	8" x 21½"
	L	1	8" x 9"

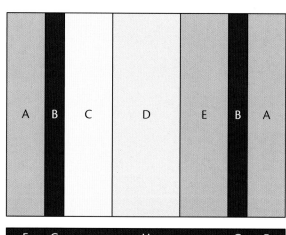

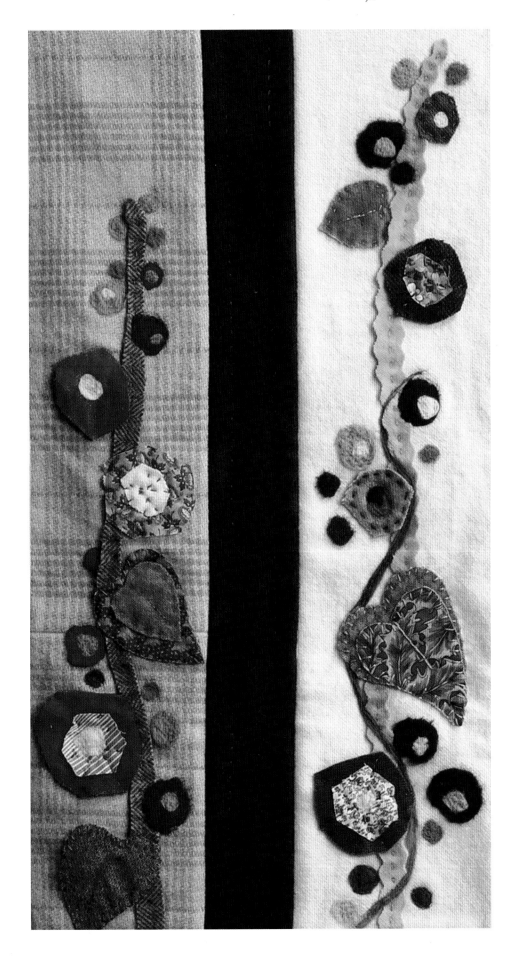

CONSTRUCTION

1. Refer to "Cutting Free-Form Strips" on page 17 for making stems. For upper blocks, cut three strips of green wool, ½" to ¾" wide and approximately 21" in length. For lower background blocks, cut three stems approximately 8" in length.

2. Referring to "Wool Rickrack" on page 16, cut three strips of green wool rickrack, ½" to ¾" wide and approximately 21" in length, for upper blocks. For lower blocks, cut three stems 8" in length. If you cannot get the length needed from your piece of wool, you can use shorter lengths and hide joined stems under appliqué or needle felting.

3. Referring to the placement guide on page 52, position the rickrack stems and random-cut stems on the background wool. Keep in mind that there is a ½" seam allowance. Pin in place. Appliqué the stems with pearl cotton using a running stitch.

4. Using variegated purple wool yarn, lightly needle felt the vine in place, following the pattern placement.

5. Make freezer-paper templates for the leaves using the pattern on page 51. Cut out the leaves from assorted green wool and green cotton fabrics. Referring to the placement guide, position the leaves and pin them in place. Using matching or contrasting pearl cotton, appliqué each leaf in place with a blanket stitch or straight stitch.

6. Make freezer-paper templates for the flowers using the patterns on page 51. Cut out the flowers from assorted wool and cotton fabrics. Referring to the pattern for placement, position the flowers and pin them in place. Some flowers are held in place by needle felting alone. Others are stitched in place with matching or contrasting pearl cotton using a blanket stitch or straight stitch. For the flowers hanging over the lattice, stitch them in place after the quilt top is sewn together.

7. Using your choice of wool-fleece colors and following the pattern for placement, first needle-felt appliqué all the wool or cotton flowers in position lightly, and then lightly needle felt the small circles and circle flowers in position. Have fun adding as many or as few hollyhock flowers on your stems as you would like. Enjoy blending, shading, and highlighting, too. Feel free to move the shapes around until you're happy with their placement and color. Then completely needle felt the fleece flowers and vine.

8. Referring to the quilt diagram on page 48 and the photo on page 47, sew all pieces together with a ½" seam allowance. Press seams open with an iron on the wool setting.

9. After the top is pieced, appliqué the hollyhock flowers that hang over the lattice.

10. Sometimes wool will stretch or embroidery will pull in the background, making the quilt top uneven. Simply trim the finished quilt top so edges are straight and corners are square. Center the quilt top on the backing fabric, allowing 3" of fabric backing around the edges to be brought around to the front for binding. We didn't use batting for this quilt. Pin baste.

11. Machine stitch or hand quilt in the ditch. Hand quilt ½" inside the lattice edges with matching pearl cotton.

12. Use the binding method described on page 20. Cut cotton backing fabric 1¼" from the quilt-top edge, and fold over the edge to meet the edge of the quilt top. Press along the fold. Place the folded edge ½" over the quilt-top edge. Pin in place. With a running stitch and matching pearl cotton, stitch to the quilt top.

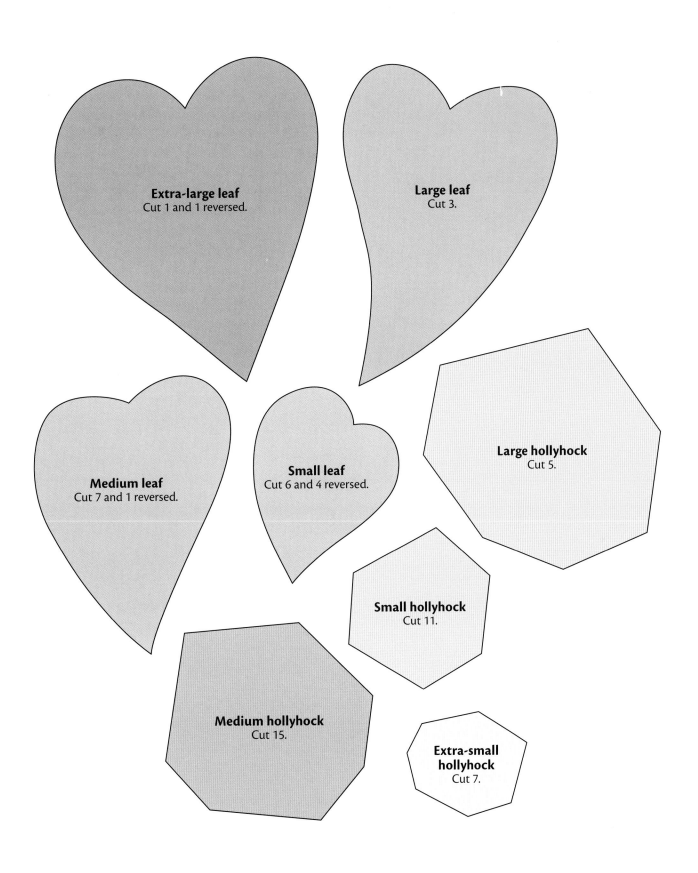

Extra-large leaf
Cut 1 and 1 reversed.

Large leaf
Cut 3.

Medium leaf
Cut 7 and 1 reversed.

Small leaf
Cut 6 and 4 reversed.

Large hollyhock
Cut 5.

Small hollyhock
Cut 11.

Medium hollyhock
Cut 15.

**Extra-small
hollyhock**
Cut 7.

Placement guide

- - - - - - - Cotton appliqué

———— Wool appliqué

〰〰〰 Felting

GARDEN FOLK-ART WALL QUILT

SIMPLE NEEDLE-FELTING TECHNIQUES MAKE THE OVERWHELMING ABUNDANCE OF BERRIES A CINCH TO CREATE. THE COMBINATION OF COTTON DECORATOR FABRICS AND THE WARMTH OF OVERDYED WOOL GIVE THIS FOLK-ART WALL QUILT A FRESH LOOK.

FINISHED SIZE: 27" X 27"

MATERIALS

1 yard of brown wool for center block, backing, and fold-over binding

Assorted wool in shades of greens, reds, and tan for border

Assorted cotton print, stripe, and plaid fabrics in coordinating shades of green, red, and tan for border

Scraps of wool in shades of red to pink for flowers

Scraps of cotton print for flower centers

Scraps of green wool for stems and vase

Pure Wool Inc.'s 100% merino fleece/roving color palette packs in *Red Rapture* and *Into the Forest*

Hand-felting needle

Straight pins

2"-thick foam work surface

#22 chenille needle

#8 pearl cotton in brown, variegated green, and shades of red to pink

Scalloped-blade and wave-blade rotary cutters, cutting mat, and ruler

CUTTING

All measurements include ½"-wide seam allowances. From brown wool and assorted red, green, and tan cotton and wool fabrics for border, cut the following pieces.			
FABRIC	**PIECE**	**NUMBER TO CUT**	**DIMENSIONS**
Brown wool	Background	1	15" x 15"
Red wool	A	1	5" x 7"
	E	1	6" x 7"
	M	1	7" x 9"
Cotton stripe	B	1	3" x 5"
	D	1	5" x 7"
	H	1	7" x 9"
Light green wool	C	1	5" x 7"
Cotton floral	F	1	5" x 7"
	J	1	7" x 7"
	N	1	9" x 11"
Green wool	G	1	6" x 7"
Dark green wool	I	1	5" x 7"
Tan wool	K	1	9" x 9"
Cotton plaid	L	1	3" x 9"

CONSTRUCTION

1. Using the template patterns on page 56, cut six flowers from pink and red wool fabrics. Cut six circles from cotton print fabrics for flower centers. Refer to "Reverse Wool Appliqué" on page 19 to reverse appliqué flower centers with a blanket stitch and matching or contrasting pearl cotton.

2. Referring to "Wool Rickrack" on page 16, cut six strips of green wool rickrack into 4" lengths. Referring to the photo on page 53 for placement, position the rickrack on the 15" brown wool background square. Pin in place. Appliqué the rickrack with a chenille needle and pearl cotton.

3. Make freezer-paper templates for the vase by using the pattern on page 56. Cut out the vase from green wool, using a scalloped-blade rotary cutter to cut across the top of the shape. Center the vase 1" from the bottom of the block and pin in place. Appliqué with green pearl cotton and a buttonhole stitch.

4. Referring to the placement guide on page 57, position the flowers and pin them in place. Using different shades of fleece from red to pink, attach the flowers to the background fabric by needle felting eight small teardrop shapes on each flower.

5. Completely needle felt four leaves in position, following the placement guide. Chain stitch stems for berries with variegated green pearl cotton.

6. Lightly needle felt berries along stems in shades of red to pink and green. When you are happy with their placement and the arrangement of color, securely needle felt all berries.

7. Referring to the quilt diagram at right and the photograph on page 53, sew the borders to the needle-felted block. Sew pieces A–C together, press the seam allowances open, and then sew this unit to the right side of the block. Sew pieces D–G together, press the seam allowances open, and then sew this unit to the top of the block. Sew pieces H–J together, press as before, and then sew this unit to the bottom of the block. Sew pieces K–N together, press, and then sew this unit to the left side of the block.

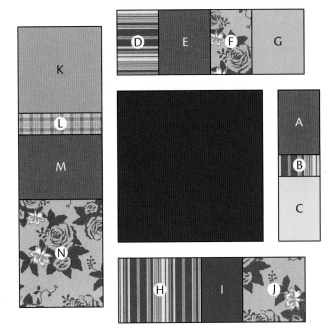

8. If the quilt top is uneven, trim the finished edges to make them straight and square the corners. Center the quilt top on the wool backing fabric, allowing 2" of fabric backing around the edges to be brought around to the front for the binding. We did not use batting in this quilt. Pin baste.

9. Machine stitch or hand quilt in the ditch. Hand quilt with red pearl cotton, stitching 1½" outside the center block. Place a French knot in the center of each flower with red pearl cotton.

10. Use the binding method described on page 21. With a scalloped blade, cut the brown wool backing fabric 1½" from the edge of the quilt. Fold the backing over to the top of the quilt edge. Pin in place. With brown pearl cotton and a blanket stitch, attach the fold-over binding, using the scalloped edge as a guide.

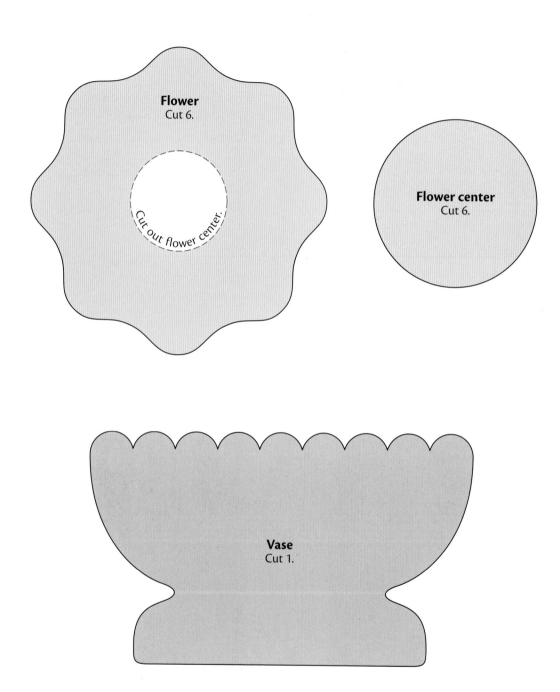

Flower
Cut 6.

Cut out flower center.

Flower center
Cut 6.

Vase
Cut 1.

Chain stitch

Placement guide

—————— Wool appliqué

— — — — Reverse appliqué

▨▨▨▨▨ Felting

SWEET BLOSSOMS MINI-QUILT

FUN COTTON STRIPES CREATE AN INTERESTING SETTING FOR PRETTY PASTEL
WOOL FLOWERS. THIS MINI-QUILT WILL BRIGHTEN ANY TABLE OR WALL.

FINISHED SIZE: 17" X 17"

MATERIALS

¾ yard of green wool fabric for backing

½ yard of striped cotton fabric for background

Nine 6" squares of wool in assorted pastel shades for flowers

Pure Wool Inc.'s 100% merino fleece/roving color palette pack in *Pastel Palette*

Hand-felting needle

2"-thick foam work surface

#22 chenille needle

#8 green pearl cotton

Scalloped-blade rotary cutter, cutting mat, and ruler

CONSTRUCTION

1. Cut nine 6" squares from the striped cotton fabric.

2. Lay out the squares in three rows of three squares each, alternating the direction of the stripes. Using a ¼" seam allowance, piece the squares together. Press the quilt top.

3. Using the template pattern on page 60, cut out nine flowers using the freezer-paper method described on page 17. With different color combinations of pastel fleece, needle felt a swirled flower center on each wool flower using the method described on page 60.

4. Center a flower on the center square of the quilt top and pin in place. The other flowers are not centered because of the fold-over binding. Pin these flowers in place leaving 1" from the outside edges of the quilt top.

5. With a chenille needle and green pearl cotton, use a running stitch to sew the wool flowers to background, stitching about ⅛" to ¼" from the edge of the flowers.

6. Center the quilt top on the wool backing fabric, allowing 2" of the wool fabric around all edges. This will eventually be brought around to the front for binding. We didn't use batting for this quilt. Pin baste.

7. Machine stitch or hand quilt in the ditch. Hand or machine stitch ½" from the quilt top edge.

8. With a scalloped rotary-cutting blade, trim the green wool backing fabric ¾" from the edges of the quilt. Fold the green backing edges over to the top of the quilt and pin in place. With green pearl cotton and a blanket stitch, attach the fold-over binding using the scalloped edge as a guide.

Simply changing the layout of the striped squares gives this mini-quilt new possibilities as a table runner.

SWIRL FLOWER TECHNIQUE

Pull a length of fleece from each of two or more colors. Lay the lengths side by side, and then hold them at both ends and twist in opposite directions. Lay the fleece on the background fabric and, starting with the end of the twisted fleece in the center of the design, coil the twisted fleece to form a swirl. Tuck the ends under the swirl and needle felt in place.

Flower
Cut 9.

RESOURCES

Pure Wool Inc.

www.pure-wool.net

1-708-601-1979

Wool fleece color palette packs,
hand-felting needles, patterns

Bernina of America Inc.

www.berninausa.com

1-630-978-2500

Machine needle-punching attachment

Clover Needlecraft, Inc.

www.clover-usa.com

Hand-felting needle tool and mats

Valdani Inc.

www.valdani.com

1-866-VALDANI (1-866-825-3264)

Hand-dyed variegated pearl cotton

Weeks Dye Works

www.weeksdyeworks.com

1-877-OVERDYE (1-877-683-7393)

Hand-dyed wool fabric and pearl cotton

ABOUT
THE AUTHORS

JENNIFER KOOY ZOETERMAN

Learn the rules and then bend them. This is Jennifer's theory concerning sewing and quilting.

Having stitched most of her life, she's known for never following a pattern to the letter, but changing it in some way to make it hers. While teaching quilters for 10 years, Jennifer helped students learn the correct techniques, but then encouraged them to put their own creative spin on things.

Jennifer incorporated her love of sewing with her imaginative outlook to cocreate Pure Wool, a resource for needle-felting fibers, supplies, and patterns. Together with her business partner, Linda Lenich, they have previously published designs in *Hooked on Wool* and *Needle Felting: Simple Techniques, Beautiful Projects,* published by Martingale.

She lives with her husband, Tim, in a Chicago suburb. Together they raised their now-adult daughters, Sara and Rachel.

LINDA LENICH

Linda believes that there must be a sewing gene passed down through her maternal DNA, because she comes from a long succession of women who loved to sew. Linda was born in Chicago and raised near the sound of her mother's sewing machine.

It was while teaching and working for many years at a local quilt shop that Linda developed an instant friendship with her coworker and future business partner, Jennifer Zoeterman. Their combined creative talents and boundless ideas are expressed in their first book, *Needle Felting: Simple Techniques, Beautiful Projects,* published by Martingale.

Linda is fascinated by the designs, textures, and colors of vintage fabrics and often wears vintage clothing or vintage accessories. She and her husband, Michael, enjoy a happy and simple life in a southern suburb of Chicago, Illinois.

NEW AND BESTSELLING TITLES FROM

Martingale®
& C O M P A N Y

America's Best-Loved Craft & Hobby Books®
America's Best-Loved Knitting Books®

That Patchwork Place®

America's Best-Loved Quilt Books®

APPLIQUÉ
Adoration Quilts
Appliqué at Play
Cutting-Garden Quilts—*NEW!*
Favorite Quilts from Anka's Treasures
Mimi Dietrich's Baltimore Basics
**Mimi Dietrich's Favorite Applique
    Quilts—*NEW!***
Sunbonnet Sue and Scottie Too
Tea in the Garden

FOCUS ON WOOL
The Americana Collection
Needle Felting
Needle-Felting Magic—*NEW!*
Simply Primitive

GENERAL QUILTMAKING
All Buttoned Up
Bits and Pieces—*NEW!*
Bound for Glory
Calendar Kids
Charmed—*NEW!*
Christmas with Artful Offerings
Colorful Quilts
Comfort and Joy
Cool Girls Quilt—*NEW!*
Creating Your Perfect Quilting Space
A Dozen Roses
Fig Tree Quilts
Follow-the-Line Quilting Designs
Follow-the-Line Quilting Designs
    Volume Two
A Fresh Look at Seasonal Quilts
**The Little Box of Quilter's Chocolate
    Desserts—*NEW!***
Modern Primitive Quilts
Points of View
Positively Postcards
Prairie Children and Their Quilts
Quilt Revival
Quilter's Block-a-Day Calendar
Quilting in the Country

Sensational Sashiko
Simple Seasons—*NEW!*
Simple Seasons Recipe Cards—*NEW!*
Simple Traditions
Twice Quilted
Young at Heart Quilts

LEARNING TO QUILT
Color for the Terrified Quilter
Happy Endings, Revised Edition
Let's Quilt!
Your First Quilt Book (or it should be!)

PAPER PIECING
300 Paper-Pieced Quilt Blocks
Easy Machine Paper Piecing
Paper-Pieced Mini Quilts
Show Me How to Paper Piece
Showstopping Quilts to Foundation Piece
Spellbinding Quilts

PIECING
40 Fabulous Quick-Cut Quilts
Better by the Dozen
Big 'n Easy
Clever Quarters, Too
Mosaic Picture Quilts—*NEW!*
New Cuts for New Quilts
Nine by Nine—*NEW!*
Sew Fun, Sew Colorful Quilts—*NEW!*
Sew One and You're Done
Snowball Quilts
Square Deal
Sudoku Quilts
Twosey-Foursey Quilts
Wheel of Mystery Quilts

QUILTS FOR BABIES & CHILDREN
Even More Quilts for Baby
Lickety-Split Quilts for Little Ones
The Little Box of Baby Quilts
Quilts for Baby
Sweet and Simple Baby Quilts

SCRAP QUILTS
Nickel Quilts
Save the Scraps
Simple Strategies for Scrap Quilts

CRAFTS
101 Sparkling Necklaces
Art from the Heart—*NEW!*
The Beader's Handbook—*NEW!*
Card Design
Creative Embellishments
Crochet for Beaders—*NEW!*
It's a Wrap
It's in the Details
The Little Box of Beaded Bracelets
    and Earrings
The Little Box of Beaded Necklaces
    and Earrings
Miniature Punchneedle Embroidery
A Passion for Punchneedle
Punchneedle Fun
Scrapbooking off the Page…
    and on the Wall
Sculpted Threads
Sew Sentimental—*NEW!*

KNITTING & CROCHET
**365 Crochet Stitches a Year:
    Perpetual Calendar—*NEW!***
365 Knitting Stitches a Year:
    Perpetual Calendar
A to Z of Knitting
Crocheted Pursenalities
First Crochet
First Knits
Fun and Funky Crochet
Handknit Skirts—*NEW!*
Handknit Style II
The Knitter's Book of Finishing
    Techniques
Knitting Circles around Socks
Knitting with Gigi
The Little Box of Crocheted Throws
The Little Box of Knitted Throws
Modern Classics
More Sensational Knitted Socks
Pursenalities
Top Down Sweaters
Wrapped in Comfort

Our books are available at bookstores and your favorite craft,
fabric, and yarn retailers. If you don't see the title you're looking for,
visit us at **www.martingale-pub.com** or contact us at:

1-800-426-3126

International: 1-425-483-3313 • **Fax:** 1-425-486-7596 • **Email:** info@martingale-pub.com